diary of an accidental arsonist

Ana Nari

BookLeaf Publishing

India | USA | UK

Presentation by *BookLeaf Publishing*

Web: www.bookleafpub.com

E-mail: info@bookleafpub.com

ISBN: 9789360945763

First edition 2024

traveling

i won't do it myself
not today.
but if you find my heart has gone,
pack your bags, take a trip.
forget the loss of the body
and track down the heart.
teach her all the things
my brain never knew.
watch her pump and bleed.
give her time.

she knows not what she was made for
only remembers beating too fast, dripping,
suffocating as i covered her
with my own two hands
it wasn't worth staying.
she knew this. i knew....

pick her up off of the ground -
show her what a real home is.

i was never one.

my heart is heavy, heavy in my chest
i can't hold the weight of it.

- A.N.

abandonment

what i find most beautiful
are the places that we have built and left behind.
a character flaw, maybe.
here is the locked gate
that was never really locked.
rusted, opens with the sound of a voice.
i don't know what it's like to go into battle
without expecting a bullet in your chest.
here i am, standing.
always ready for the war;
never for the tsunami.

- A.N.

the art of it all

whatever it is you wanted
has been canceled.
but there's something in its likeness
standing at that street corner
and it's waiting for you.
come closer, it says
reach out.
walk with me
to the ends of the earth.
look -
but don't touch.

please,
leave me stranded in the rain
with no way of getting home, shadow
i need a dramatic moment
for my poetry
and watch me break apart at midnight, shadow.
it's good for my notes on a mind deprived
of affection, connection.

watch me put myself back together
in the morning
with a corner piece missing
and with a sky grayer than i remember

don't say a thing.
it's good for me
i write better for it.
teach me the art of detachment, shadow
show me how to reject vulnerability
from my body
like it's a foreign object.

and don't wish me well.
this, right here,
is cathartic.

- A.N.

lighthouse

there's an incandescent light somewhere
in this abandoned lighthouse.
i have not yet found it.
last night, it got too dark for me to see,
so i lit myself on fire.

- A.N.

storm drain

it was monday when she fell through the cracks.
it was wednesday when she gave in
to the storm drain snowflakes.
bitter, broken, beautiful.
dirty.
we've not seen her since.
oh, don't look at me [like that].
i don't know why I'm here, really.
i just write tragedies. and you.
today, you're an apple tree,
a puzzle not yet solved.
i fear your solidity -
let me paint you abstract.
i've never felt like this [this much].
i fear your wholeness, so let me break you
into parts i can swallow.
and let me give you a story.
this time, you're the sailor.
do you feel that?
it's the sea, it's me,
don't reach too far in, don't reach too deep.
or, you're the siren
and the song
but i'm already dead in the water
so there's no need for you.

i fear your treachery,
so i take in your aura like it's candy,
like it's a fairytale,
breadcrumbs to something i reach for in my
sleep.
ten more steps to the witch's cottage.
i enter by choice.

- A.N.

pretty girl

you know what it's like
to be loved
eyes twinkling in the summer sun
like precious metals, he tells you, right,
as he leans into you,
breathless.
tell me, pretty girl,
are there secrets to be found there?
does he wish to know all?

pretty girl,
your hair...
like rivers, waves
lovely tosses, lovely flips.

but pretty girl,
in the mirror
do you ever see me?

because sometimes i see you.

- A.N.

stroll

it makes me sick sometimes
thinking that there's a treadmill
where my heart should be.

and i wanna say "mama, i'm sick"
but it doesn't matter
i know what you'd tell me.

but i'm pretty from a distance
here on the outskirts
and exactly where i belong.
can you still see me here?
am i blurry enough to love?

there are always cars
so many damn cars
everywhere, always
with too many turn signals
and benches of love
not for me, not for me.
and heads in hands -
i'm sorry i couldn't help you,
i've forgotten how to speak.

why am i so afraid

of everything,
all the time.
3 am and my hearts still running, sprinting
the 100-meter dash
stop! you don't want love, dear.
you're going in the wrong direction.

i see the signs of a person transformed.
wake me up when i get there.

- A.N.

haunting

yesterday this room was full
yesterday there was no one in this room
but the ghosts.
and it was louder than it's ever been.
and i begged for forgiveness at an altar
that no longer exists.

- A.N.

ambulance

sirens scream somewhere outside
then drift further away
as things do.

the television grows louder
my father's voice grows louder.
and i, silent, atop a flight of stairs, listen
to the siren sounds fading
marking a tragedy i may never know.
i look down at my hands trembling
and my feet tapping to some invisible beat
crafted just for this kind of fear.
i hallucinate a victory
a sword and a stone
and i can no longer hear the ambulance.

i would like
one day
to be selfless.

- A.N.

black hole

welcome to the void.
isn't it better, this?
to be numb?
alone is what you have known longest,
it's what makes you
(comfortable).
you know this story well
but still,
the boy with the angel smile,
the red-lipped girl who smiled back.

and you (aren't you here too?)

- A.N.

wartime

so this is what we have created.
humanity:
led lights and war.

ask me how i'm doing,
and i'll tell you that the subway i built for
myself still works.
but i still don't know what it's like to be
comfortable.
paint peels, faces blur.
the train doesn't stop.

i'll tell you that even during war,
i take the mess of dust and stars
and paint beauty,
poetry,
one and the same.
i'll tell you that sometimes, to pass the time,
i drink the blood of my dying aspirations,
so serotonin tastes like copper today.
i'll tell you
that i don't know what it's like
to be whole.

forgive me.

- A.N.

we wanted to swim

it's funny
how water only seems beautiful
when you're not drowning in it
when it's not slowing your breath to a stop
when sharks don't thirst for your blood
and expect it to come easy
you reach out
one last time before it pulls you under.
somehow it's comforting -
and you think, maybe you want this.
maybe you've wanted this all along.

- A.N.

diary of an accidental arsonist

there are snake-headed things
in the darkest corners of the night.
alive only with the neon signs.
some starry sins.
when you finally make it home, dear,
give my best to penelope -
she's waited long.
a candle, lit somewhere in the distance.
for a moment,
light flickers;
faces glow, blurry.
alone with my thoughts, once more
at home with the undercurrent.

nostalgia always makes its way
into my modern dreams.
i dream of them (forgive the obscurity)
in a florida mall.
i dream of them dancing
through empty parking lots
i've never visited.
but i know them all well.

i keep building fire escapes with my fingers
as i burn my buildings to the ground.

it's all in the making of.
and i'm sorry i left the stove on.
i've learned, i really have.
i even have the marks to prove it -
i can show them to you.

and sometimes
i don't want to blow out the candles all at once.

...and the match slipped.
i have a hard time holding on to things -
give me a few friends, you'll see.
but what isn't temporary?

the burn mark on my arm
started acting up again.
it said, "do you remember the flames?"
"do you see them, even now?"
"even now," i parrot back.

even now.

- A.N.

an understatement

i pull my knees up to my chest
in different ways,
curl up in on myself
in different time zones;
ode to the rain that never came.
here, now, is a silence laced with truths
no one wants to hear.
here is a conversation
filled with fairytale naïveté;
he told her he loved her and she believed him.
i don't know what that's like.
i'm a little bloody
(soaked in blood).
forgive me.
i understate.
it helps with the nausea.
please forgive the blood,
the taste of copper in your mouth.
forgive the blood on your walls
and on the soles of your feet.
there's too much of me everywhere i look now.
and i'm sorry
that all i am is a minefield.
i was never taught to be anything else.

- A.N.

moat

i mourn the loss
of everything i wish for
but cannot have.

there's a moat... around...
sorry, yes, there's a moat around
my palace of desire
and he looks like that.
but it's alright -
he'll be good for my poetry.
he'll be good for my...

there are alligators.
why? you don't want me.
believe me.
i'm saving you from yourself.

she's deep in the woods
she's gorgeous,
most beautiful thing you've ever seen.

i'm releasing the drawbridge now.
you can bring your princess in -
it's getting cold out.

- A.N.

fantasyland

smiling face
and smiling eyes.

oh, dream girl
look at you!
at last, at love.
iron, not mire
with a love spun as good as gold

no longer in the land of milk
and missed opportunities
all the king's horses and all the king's men
watched you fall,
but a prince was there to catch you.

somewhere in your mind, a whisper -
love should be big enough to hold a life.

i am not comfortable where i cannot hide.

but he's a blessing -
both virtue and vice.

- A.N.

in which nothing mattered,
but everything hurt

you remember this.
twelve bars this time.
like morphine, but a little louder.

and if you fall,
fall slowly,
lightly,
or not at all.

the door shuts,
locks behind me -
and my body screams "no, no, no."
God hoping i'll learn
or the devil begging me to burn.

i don't like not hearing words
that i used to know the meaning of
but have since forgot.
histrionic, gestalt, maudlin
intimacy.

- A.N.

at a loss

how can you feel the loss of someone
before you've lost them
how can you feel a memory never made
drift in the wind
somewhere in the midst of a skyscraper,
a playlist of songs you'll never hear,
people you'll never get the chance to love.
i feel their shadows dance through my bones.
i take a breath -
a few, actually,
in rapid succession.
why am i choking?

why have i lost my own air?
why do i run my hands over my ribcage and feel
loss,
a video playing on loop -
loss.

i come back to the surface
right before asphyxiation this time.
give me a moment to breathe.

what have i lost?

what is there left of me?

i liked being there with you.
even if i wasn't, really.

- A.N.

beanstalk

there's a beanstalk in my mind
and one day i'll have to climb it.
already too many blisters
from monkey bars or bottle caps
both done alone, both while determined.
a mermaid on mulch, trampled
by six sprinting pirates
and now, teetering
on a balance-beam stretching
as far as the eye can see

no one is watching
but i've made it to the end now.
i'm safe!
is anyone home?
there's a beanstalk
and a giant, and a golden goose,
but first,
two boys on bikes,
circling, laughing,
and three green stars,
only when i turn off the lights.

will someone stay here
and wait with me?

it's raining
and i'm back where i started
raining
and there's no one here.
i'm soaked now, shivering

no one here.
i deserve this.
and there's no one
i deserve.
there's a beanstalk in my mind.

one day, it won't be there anymore.

- A.N.

kraken

they're here now, aren't they?
the dark, ugly things
sweeping through your soul,
like the creatures you hear about
in sailor's tales.
don't look at them,
and maybe they'll be kind enough
to rip you apart quickly.
count to ten,
and pretend you're hallucinating.
this isn't happening to you.
count to twenty,
and you'll wash up on sand, soaking, breathless.
count to thirty,
and find land again.

\- A.N.

recurring themes

if there's a bush
and it's in flames
but not burning up
do i move towards it
or back away

and if the trees are screaming,
"not for you, not for you"
but there's still a bush
and still it's on fire
and still calling
what shall i do, Lord?
what shall i do?

- A.N.